# concise
# notes
# on
# software
# engineering

# concise
# notes
# on
# software
# engineering

**by tom de marco**

**A YOURDON Press Monograph**

1133 Avenue of the Americas, New York, N.Y. 10036

Printed in the United States of America

Library of Congress Catalog Number 79-66408

ISBN: 0-917072-16-2

This book was set in Times Roman by YOURDON Press, 1133 Avenue of the Americas, New York, N.Y., using a PDP-11/45 running under the UNIX operating system.

# contents

# concise notes on software engineering

# 0: preface

During the past ten years, the application of basic engineering methods to software system building has resulted in a number of new system development disciplines:

1. Structured Analysis

2. Software Tools (Component Assembly)

3. Structured Design

4. Walkthroughs

5. Data-Driven Design

6. Information-Hiding

7. Pseudocode

8. Structured Coding

9. Top-Down Implementation

10. Software Metrics

In combination, these ten disciplines often are referred to as "software engineering."

The purpose of *Concise Notes* is to provide definitions, notations, history, and principal references on each of the software engineering disciplines. It is not my intention herein to *teach* anything, but rather to refresh your memory on what you may already have learned, or to direct you properly in pursuit of more information.

## Organization

*Concise Notes* is organized by discipline, with one chapter allocated to each discipline. The order of the chapters approximately represents the order in which the treated disciplines become relevant and useful over the course of a project. Within each chapter, if appropriate, there are sections pertaining to

- guiding principles
- rationale
- definitions
- conventions
- annotated list of key works

## References

The Bibliography contains a complete reference for each cited source. The references are ordered by a key made up of the first three characters of the first-listed author's name, followed by a unique digit. Thus, Yourdon and Constantine's *Structured Design* is referred to as [YOU-7]. These reference keys are used throughout, always enclosed in square brackets.

## Assurances of the Author's Utter Objectivity

I have made no great effort in these pages to be totally objective. There is such a large body of published work in the area of software engineering, and so much of it is unreadable, unrealistic, and crushingly dull, that I have pruned mention of it down to a select few. In annotating references and in choosing which ones to mention, I have used my own judgment and opinion. Where there are several conventions or notations in common use, I have selected one for inclusion, and merely referenced the others.

Throughout *Concise Notes,* I have worked under the premise that presentation of a coherent and comprehensible subset of the possibilities would be more useful than an exhaustive (and exhausting) treatment.

# 1: structured analysis

Structured Analysis involves the use of function networks and supporting tools to develop an analysis-phase model of a system. The discipline of Structured Analysis dates from the early 1970s. Prior to that time, many of the concepts of Structured Analysis had been used piecemeal [WHI-1, TEI-2, COU-1]. The first reports of conscious use of Structured Analysis as an integrated approach to analysis were published in 1976 [YOU-3 and ROS-1].

## 1.1 Principles of Structured Analysis

- □ Construct system models using the three tools of Structured Analysis:

  - Data Flow Diagrams (DFDs)
  - Data Dictionary
  - Structured English

- □ Use the system models to facilitate communication with the users.

- □ Incorporate into the system specification (Structured Specification) a model of the system to be implemented.

- □ Limit the specification so as to deal only with the completed model — plus minimal overhead. This will assure that the factors listed at the top of the following page occur:

- reduce redundancy and bulk

- enhance specification maintainability

- eliminate busy-work of narrative description

## 1.2 Rationale for Structured Analysis

The major advantage of Structured Analysis is that it helps analysts and users come to a more accurate, early understanding of what the new system will be and how it will fit into their business. This means fewer surprises during acceptance testing, and substantially reduces the flurry of user-requested changes during the first few months of system operation. This more formal approach to preparing the specification has some further advantages for the analyst:

- a concrete and well-defined set of analysis-phase tasks and deliverables

- a physically smaller specification (typically less than a third the size of a classical functional specification)

- iterative approaches, involving minimal overhead per iteration

- savings of time that otherwise would be spent producing narrative, soon-outdated documentation

## 1.3 Definitions of Structured Analysis Terms

A DATA FLOW DIAGRAM is a network representation of a system. It portrays the system in terms of its component parts. Figure 1.1, on the facing page, shows an abstract Data Flow Diagram.

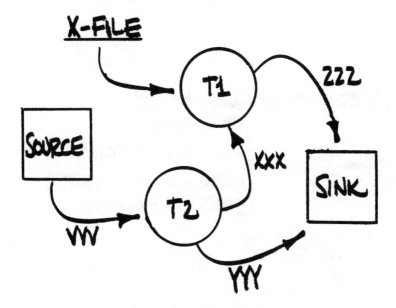

Figure 1.1: Data flow diagram.

A Data Flow Diagram is made up of four elements: *dataflows, transforms, data stores,* and *terminators.*

A *dataflow* is a conduit through which packets of information of known composition flow. The vector XXX in Figure 1.1 represents a dataflow.

A *transform* is a process that converts one or more incoming dataflows into outgoing dataflow(s). In the figure, bubbles T1 and T2 represent transforms.

A *data store* is a time-delayed repository of information (X-FILE in the figure). Data stores can be thought of as manual or automated files or databases or any other accumulation of data.

A *terminator* is a net originator or receiver of system data (SOURCE and SINK in Figure 1.1 are terminators). Its purpose is to mark the boundary of a model, that is, the edge of the area of interest. Terminators are used to represent people, organizations, and systems just beyond the system context boundary.

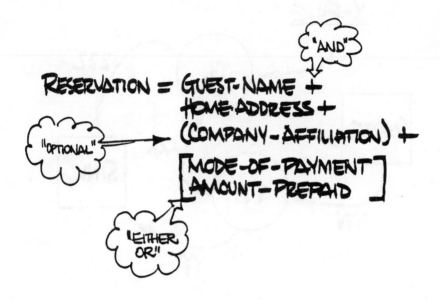

Figure 1.2:  Sample data dictionary definition.

DATA DICTIONARY is a set of definitions of interfaces declared in the model.  Definitions in the Data Dictionary represent dataflows and data stores in terms of their components.  A sample definition is presented in Figure 1.2 above.  Components may themselves be dataflows, or they may be *data elements*.

> A *data element* is a primitive dataflow, that is, one that has no meaningful components.

A MINISPEC is a description of user policy governing a particular transform declared in the model.  Usually there is one minispec for each primitive (that is, a transform that is not further partitioned).  Minispecs are written using such tools as decision tables, decision trees, and *Structured English.*

> *Structured English* is an English language subset that utilizes a limited vocabulary (mostly Data Dictionary-defined terms) and a limited syntax.  An indentation convention is used to call attention to subordination. Figure 1.3 presents a sample policy described in Structured English.

FOR EACH CUSTOMER ON FILE :
   ACCUMULATE CUST-BAL INTO DEBIT-TOTAL
   IF CYCLE-DATE = TODAYS-DATE
      PRINT CUSTOMER-NAME ON
      TODAYS-CALL-LIST

   MARK DATE-LAST-PROCESSED =
   TODAYS-DATE

Figure 1.3:  Sample minispec.

A SYSTEM MODEL is an integrated set of Data Flow Diagrams, Data Dictionary, and minispecs used to specify a system or a portion of one.  Figure 1.4 describes the model, and shows the correlations among components.

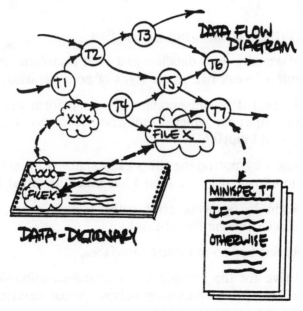

Figure 1.4:  System model.

## 1.4 Conventions of Structured Analysis

**DFD CONVENTIONS:**

**Notation:**

See Figure 1.5. Other notations are described in [GAN-3 and SOF-1].

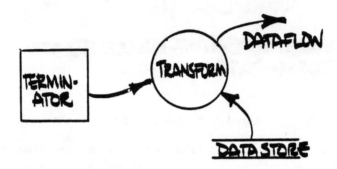

**Figure 1.5: DFD notation.**

**Procedure:**

1.   Portray dataflow, not control flow.

2.   Make sure each dataflow and each transform are nameable — weak names are signs of poor partitioning.

3.   Respect data conservation. No transform can produce an output for which it does not have access to the required input(s).

4.   Begin by portraying the steady state. Add startup and closedown after the model has taken its initial shape.

5.   Begin by ignoring error paths (simply mark them as REJECT for the time-being).

6.   Repartition to minimize interfaces.

7.   Strive for the minimally connected partitioned presentation of the underlying policy. Avoid describing how the requirement will be met.

**Leveling:**

Where subject matter will not fit comfortably onto a single sheet, or diagram is overly complex, use leveled DFDs. (See Figure 1.6.) Make sure that:

- child and parent diagrams are in *balance,* i.e., input and output dataflows shown at a bubble on the parent are equivalent to inputs and outputs at the corresponding child figure.

- data stores are declared at the highest level where they are accessed by two or more transforms.

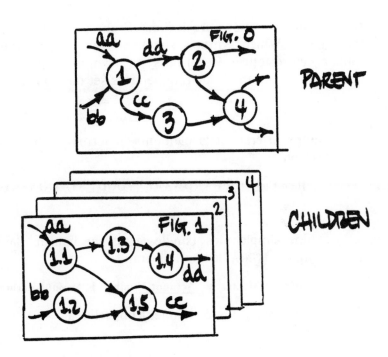

Figure 1.6: The leveled set.

**DATA DICTIONARY CONVENTIONS:**

1.  Define all data stores and dataflows used on the DFD set. Define any subordinate dataflows used in other definitions.

2.  Use the operators

> \+   meaning   AND
> [ ]  meaning   SELECT ONE OF
> { }  meaning   ITERATIONS OF

**Examples**

Account-Record       =   Account-Description + {Sales-Item}
Account-Description  =   Account-Holder-Name + Address + Status
Sales-Item           =   Date + [ Item-Code | Item-Description ] + Amount

Note: Other notations are legion. Each is incompatible with all the others. Which symbols you use is not so important if you remain consistent. Regardless of symbols, try to restrict definitions to the three logical operators set out above.

3.  Define discrete data elements in terms of the values they take on:

> Item-Code = [ HARDWARE | FOOD | STATIONERY ]

4.  Define simple files (single-access mechanism data stores) using the ITERATIONS OF operator:

> Account-Master = {<u>Account-Number</u> + Account-Record}

with the accessing component underlined.

5.  Define multi-access data stores in terms of component, simple files. Use a Data Structure Diagram [DEM-3] or a subschema [MAR-1] to show how the components combine to make the whole. (See Figure 1.7 on the facing page.) Define component simple files with the Data Dictionary operators.

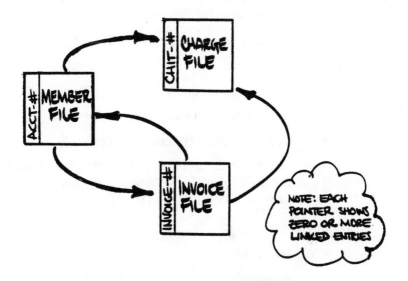

**Figure 1.7: Data structure diagram.**

6.  Order Data Dictionary entries alphabetically by item name.

7.  When backward access is required, search entire Data Dictionary if no automated facility is available. Since backward access is fairly rare, this almost always is preferable to paying the price of multiple entries for each new definition and each modification.


**MINISPEC CONVENTIONS:**

1.  Write one minispec for each functional primitive (bottom-level transform).

2.  Describe user policy governing the transform. Avoid describing any particular implementation of policy.

3.  Select a descriptive method tailored to the policy being described. (Don't try to select one method for all.)

4.  Favor non-procedural methods (tables, graphs, figures, decision tables) where applicable.

5.  If the minispec goes beyond a single page, consider partitioning the transform further.

**STRUCTURED ENGLISH CONVENTIONS:**

1.  Limit vocabulary to

    - nouns and modifier from Data Dictionary
    - imperative transitive verbs
    - numbers and numeric qualifiers
    - other words necessary to construct logical formulations (for example: IF, CASE, OTHERWISE, EQUAL, LESS THAN)

2.  Avoid the following:

    - adverbs
    - punctuation
    - compound sentences

3.  Combine Structured English statements and statement groups using only the following mechanisms:

    - simple sequence
    - repeated set with conditions of repetition clearly stated at the top of the set
    - conditional set(s) with the condition of application clearly stated at the top

4.  Use indentation to show subordination of statement groups to any condition that governs them. See Figure 1.8.

```
For each Customer-Order:
     Save Order-# and Date on Journal
     Fetch Customer-Record of Customer-#
     If found
          Add Order-Total to Customer-Total
          Set Customer-Activity-Date = Today's Date
          Add Order-Total to Customer-Total
     Otherwise (invalid Customer-#)
          Save Customer-Order on Error-Log
```

Figure 1.8: Structured English Minispec.

## 1.5  Source Material on Structured Analysis

Source material on Structured Analysis includes three texts, a number of relevant papers, and an audio-visual training course. In addition, there are seminars available from the three principal developers of the method: YOURDON inc., SofTech, and Improved Systems Technology. Among the published works, the following should be noted:

DeMarco [DEM-3] provides a complete description of the method of Structured Analysis, justification for its use, and a case-study example. This is a valuable work, somewhat marred by the author's sophomoric attempts at humor and his inexcusable irreverence toward the major institutions of our industry.

Gane and Sarson [GAN-3] cover the same ground as [DEM-3], but with a slightly different point of view and a completely different case study. The major differences between [DEM-3] and this work are in the areas of Data Dictionary and use of Structured Analysis tools to develop a formal specification. An excellent and highly readable presentation of the material.

*IEEE Transactions on Software Engineering,* January 1977 [REF-1], is a collection of articles from different sources on the subject of Structured Analysis. It is most valuable for its presentation of SADT, an approach to Structured Analysis advocated by SofTech Inc. In the light of SofTech's all-important early work in Structured Analysis, these articles are particularly significant.

Teichroew [TEI-1 and TEI-2] describes work on the now-famous ISDOS project in the development of automated aids for system analysis. This work took place at the University of Michigan starting in the early 1970s.

Selected papers by Structured Analysis users [SIM-1 and KAI-1] describe experience with the concepts of Structured Analysis in large commercial organizations.

Many of the ideas central to Structured Analysis (such as, hierarchical network modeling during planning stages, minimization of interfaces, flow diagrams) are common in other technical disciplines. In the field of architecture, an approach that is remarkably like Structured Analysis is described by Alexander [ALE-1].

# 2: software tools (component assembly)

There is nothing new about the idea of using existing software instead of writing fresh code for each new application. The problems associated with the idea aren't new either:

- It's often harder to find existing code than to write your own.

- Modifying someone else's code can be tiresome and frustrating.

What *is* new over the past few years is that more and more people are making the concept work. This trend has taken two forms: Individuals build their own personal libraries of reusable code; or, organizations make sizable investments in component libraries.

## 2.1 Principles of Component Assembly

☐ Develop a set of highly cohesive modular building blocks.

☐ Use these component modules at the bottom of the design hierarchy.

☐ Assemble as much of the system as possible using components.

## 2.2 Rationale for Component Assembly

Typically, the majority of modules in a hierarchy are at the bottom level. Avoiding new development for a substantial percentage of these (a third?) can increase net productivity enormously. Small, highly cohesive, primitive modules tend to be reusable as a natural consequence of strong cohesion. The added cost increment to make the module reusable can be offset by re-use factors of ten or more. (Some of the building blocks in use at YOURDON inc. are combined literally dozens of times per week into new applications!)

## 2.3 A Caveat

Before you get re-excited by this very old idea, let's examine why it doesn't work when it doesn't work, and why it does work when it does. Major reasons for failure in the past to develop usable component libraries include

- unwillingness to invest in tools

- underestimation of the cost (and value) of reusability

- lack of understanding of what constituted a useful component

- lack of homogeneity in design methods (So the kinds of components one designer might find useful were of little value to another.)

- over-reliance on CPU vendors to supply tools (They'd really rather we'd start afresh each time.)

Reasons for recent success with the concept include these:

- increasing convergence of design methods

- steady accumulation over the years of recognized useful components

- advent of operating systems that facilitate component assembly (The principal example of this trend is the Bell System's UNIX[†] operating system [REF-5].)

---

[†]UNIX is a Trademark of Bell Laboratories. The UNIX operating system is available under license from Western Electric, Greensboro, N.C.

While CPU vendors have still not come up with much, time-sharing vendors have been more active. The typical user of a time-sharing system today does virtually no programming. Almost all his system use involves packages and tools supplied by the vendor.

## 2.4 Source Material on Component Assembly

If you managed to install a usable component library in your organization, and if your programmers assembled components to build application systems, your work environment would become, effectively, a "Programmer's Workbench." That is exactly what Bell Laboratories has endeavored to establish at the Piscataway, N.J., UNIX facility. The most encouraging work on the concept of component assembly for software development has been an offshoot of Bell's Programmer's Workbench project:

> The Second International IEEE Conference on Software Engineering [REF-4] devoted an entire session to the Programmer's Workbench project. Six papers presented there describe the PWB from various developers' and users' points of view.

> Kernighan and Plauger [KER-2] provide an extended description of most of the tools used in the PWB. Their lucid (and charming) book presents the tools themselves, the philosophy for their use, and elegant source code implementations.

# 3: structured design

Structured Design is a hierarchical, interface-oriented approach to modular decomposition of software systems. As a formal discipline, it owes most to the early work of Larry Constantine. The concept began to evolve in the early seventies [STE-1]. Structured Design includes methods for deriving, refining, and representing modular structures.

## 3.1 Principles of Structured Design

☐ Decompose a system into modules.

☐ Arrange modules into a hierarchy.

☐ Represent hierarchy and decomposition with a structure chart.

☐ Annotate the structure chart to show coupling.

☐ Refine so as to reduce coupling, eliminate pathological connections, increase cohesion, and smooth progression from abstraction at the top to details at the bottom.

## 3.2 Definitions of Structured Design Terms

A STRUCTURE CHART is a tree-like graphic that represents the control hierarchy of a system. (See Figure 3.1 on the following page.) Subordination on a structure chart means control or use of the subordinate routine by its manager. Module A, in Figure 3.1, calls B, C, and D one or more times each. Module B calls E, F, and G.

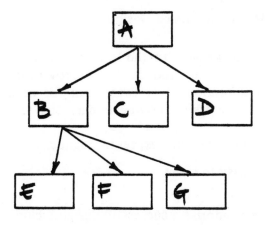

**Figure 3.1: Structure chart.**

A CONNECTION is any reference from the inside of a module to something defined outside.

A *normal connection* is a reference to another module by name (CALL, PERFORM, DO).

A *pathological control connection* is a reference (GOTO) to any secondary entry point defined in another module.

A *pathological data connection* is a reference to data defined in another module but not explicitly shared (passed) along a normal connection.

A COUPLE is a data item shared between two modules.

A *computational couple* is a shared data item used by the receiving module as a basis of calculation or indexing, but not for decision-making.

A *switching couple* is a shared data item that dictates a decision to be made by the receiving module.

COHESION is a measure of the strength of association of functions performed in or managed by a module. It is an indication of the module's justification for existence, its black-box characteristic, and of its likely reusability.

## 3.3  Rationale for Structured Design

Design is successful to the extent that it minimizes the total life-time cost of the product. Most software money goes for testing and modification of software, not for original development [BOE-1]. Successful designs are characterized as follows:

- flexible with respect to unanticipated change

- easy to test

The factors that comprise a successful design include:

- readability

- small module size

- modular independence

- black-box factor (module can be understood from without — in terms of the inputs and the outputs)

- close association between design and requirement

Structured Design is an empirically derived approach for maximizing such factors.

## 3.4  Conventions of Structured Design

Notational conventions for Structured Design are illustrated by Figure 3.2. Module A calls modules B, C, and D (normal connections) one or more times each. In calling B, A passes the couple M1 and receives back the couple M2. Both are computational couples as indicated by the open-tailed couple symbol. Module A receives a switching couple M3 back from its call to C; C contains a pathological control connection to D (a GOTO to some location inside D). D has a pathological data connection to A; it overwrites A's private data item, M4.

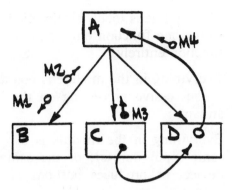

**Figure 3.2: Structure chart notation.**

Conventions for refining and improving the modular structure include the following:

1. *Reduce coupling* by moving functions among modules, combining or further decomposing modules, or regrouping into a modified hierarchy. In reducing coupling, developers should be aware of the following considerations:

   - Switches cause more coupling than computational couples.

   - Upward-passing switches are worse than downward.

   - Pathological control connections should be completely eliminated.

   - Pathological data connections should be avoided, even connections to COMMON data areas.

   - The more data elements contained in a compound couple, the worse the coupling.

2. *Test cohesion* by applying name tests (strong verb + single object names imply good cohesion; wishy-washy names imply poor cohesion).

3.    *Increase cohesion* by composing modules that pass one or more of these tests:

- The module is totally single-minded. It performs one function only, and performs that function entirely.

- Everything in the module is bound together by successive processing on the same data stream.

- Everything in the module is driven by the same input item(s), or the same complex device, or produces portions of the same output.

- The module can be completely understood in terms of parameters passed to it and received back from it.

## 3.5  Source Material on Structured Design

Yourdon and Constantine's *Structured Design* [YOU-7] is the major work on the subject, providing a complete and readable presentation of the material, and containing numerous examples.

Myers' *Reliable Software Through Composite Design* [MYE-3] is a useful second source, and is best for its discussion of coupling.

# 4: walkthroughs

Walkthroughs elicit and encourage peer review of the products of development. Their purpose is early and relatively inexpensive error removal. A by-product of the use of walkthroughs can be a growing feeling of team responsibility for the products under review.

## 4.1 Principles of Walkthroughs

□ Schedule formal review of design products and untested code.

□ Conduct the review according to a fixed, published agenda.

□ Solicit critical discussion from the reviewers for the following categories:

- hard faults
- deviation from previously agreed upon practice (standards, naming, style, and so forth)
- weakness of concept
- avoidable testing difficulties

## 4.2 Rationale for Walkthroughs

The concept of desk-checking as a part of the classical life cycle was valid in principle, but never was done. Walkthroughs not only detect errors in advance of testing, but encourage developers to think out their ideas more completely before review. The result is that more debugging is done on paper, less on the machine. Procedures for peer review provide the following advantages:

- detecting problems earlier

- spreading familiarity and expertise

- homogenizing style and method

Institution of walkthroughs has a further effect of breaking down the attitude that a program is the very private personal property of the developer, really no one else's business. By the time the walkthrough is complete, reviewers have been co-opted into considering the product as much theirs as the original developer's.

The psychological orientation of a walkthrough is highly conducive to error detection. Reviewers initially have little emotional stake in the product under review, so they are less inclined to cognitive dissonance: the failure to notice something they don't want to notice.

## 4.3 Conventions of Walkthroughs

Originally, the walkthrough involved presentation by the developer. There is a growing feeling among practitioners, however, that the product under review ought to speak for itself. In place of presentation, it is now more common for the product to be distributed enough in advance for reviewers to have studied it before the walkthrough.

Walkthroughs are conducted according to a formal set of rules, known to all parties. Suggested rules for walkthroughs appear on the following page.

## RULES FOR WALKTHROUGHS

1. Time limit = 20 minutes.

2. Number of reviewers = 3.

3. The chairperson (anyone but the developer) is in charge, ruling the procedures dictatorially.

4. No interruptions by anyone but the chairperson.

5. The walkthrough proceeds through three phases:

   - questions and answers

   - reviewers' critique (limited to enumeration of problems — no discussion of potential solutions)

   - decision to accept, accept conditionally, or reject the product

6. One participant writes informal minutes.

7. Walkthroughs are conducted on design products and then again on code.

Different organizations adopt very different conventions for walkthroughs. One extreme approach is the idea of *zero defect development*. Under this scheme, code reviews are conducted in advance of compilation. The stated goal is to remove *all* defects. (Sometimes this goal needs to be stated to break down the presumption that it is perfectly reasonable to catch half the bugs now and the rest during testing.) After review, the product is compiled. Compilation errors are recorded and tracked as an indication of continuing effectiveness of the walkthroughs. Subsequently detected bugs also are recorded. Advantages of this approach are given below:

- feedback to avoid increasing sloppiness in walkthroughs

- change of attitude — there are no "permissible bugs"

- elimination of blind spots encouraged by the compiler's "stamp of approval"

Some organizations try to gain the advantages of walkthroughs without the costs by insisting that all development products be worked on by two or more developers. A module, for instance, is coded by one person and then rotated to someone else. The second developer is encouraged to treat the product as his own, modifying and improving it until he is pleased to have it associated with his name.

## 4.4 Source Material on Walkthroughs

Weinberg's *Psychology of Computer Programming* [WEI-2] provides some of the intellectual underpinnings of the walkthrough concept. It also gives insight into reasons walkthroughs can fail, some productive and counterproductive approaches to debugging, and means to encourage a healthy sense of team development.

Fagan's "Design and Code Inspections to Reduce Errors in Program Development" [FAG-1] is a set of formal procedures for code walkthroughs and a report on experience with their use. It is a good presentation of IBM's view of the subject.

Yourdon's *Structured Walkthroughs* [YOU-5] is a how-to book on instituting and running walkthroughs.

# 5: data-driven design

Should a system or program design derive its structure from the functions performed, or from the data processed? Over the years, this question has separated design thinkers into two schools. Since data often is better defined than function at the beginning of a project, the idea of data-driven design is rather attractive: It offers the hope of a mechanistic approach to design, one that would make the process much less of an art than it usually is.

## 5.1 Principles of Data-Driven Design

☐ Determine structure of the major input and output data streams.

☐ Describe data structure in terms of sequence, iteration, and selection.

☐ Make design structure conform to structure of data processed.

## 5.2 Rationale for Data-Driven Design

The major advantage of data-driven design is that it is *mechanistic*. Two designers working on the same problem will converge upon the same answer. Maintenance programmers, to the extent that they understand the method, will be able to derive a good understanding of the design from analysis of the data. Programs will be designed exactly as the maintainer would have designed them. Thus, they will be easier to maintain.

A case also can be made based on the concept that data-driven designs are the natural extension of the idea of accommodating design to requirement. Certain data structures are handled very naturally by designs patterned upon the data structure. (See the examples given in Section 5.3.) Designs that flagrantly disregard data structure sometimes result in particularly convoluted coding problems.

## 5.3 Conventions of Data-Driven Design

In order to begin the data-driven approach, we need some way to model data structure. The possibilities include tree structures, Warnier diagrams, and Data Dictionary operators. Since I already have introduced Data Dictionary operators, I will again use them to illustrate data-driven design.

The data-structure-derived design can be applied at the micro level (to shape module internals) or at the macro level (to determine decomposition into modules). Let's begin with a micro example: Suppose a module is required to print out a report of the following form:

Tax-Report = Taxpayer-ID + {Earnings-Report} + Summary

working from an input structured very similarly:

Taxpayer-Record = Taxpayer-ID + {Earnings-Record}

In such a case, sections of the code can be combined in a fashion analogous to the data structure shown by the pseudocode of Figure 5.1. Note that a repetition structure is used to deal with the iterated portion of the data structure. Sections of code that deal with proceedings, and sections that follow concatenated data segments (for example, Taxpayer-ID and Summary) are concatenated ahead of and behind the repetition.

Figure 5.1: Data-driven design.

To reflect data structure in code formulation, apply the following rules, which are summarized by Figure 5.2.

1.  Use concatenated code sections to deal with concatenated data sections.

2.  Use IF-THEN-ELSE or CASE to deal with SELECT-ONE-OF type data structures.

3.  Use DO-WHILE or its equivalent to deal with ITERATIONS-OF type data structures.

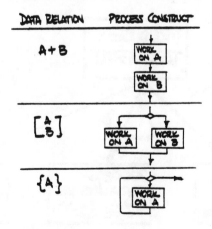

Figure 5.2: Data related to process.

With more complex data structures or where processing on the data segments is more complex, a macro use of the data-driven design concept is required. For instance, a program required to produce this output:

Tax-Report = Taxpayer-Name + {Earnings-Report} + Summary

from inputs of

Earnings-File = {Taxpayer-ID + Employer-ID + Amount}

and

Taxpayer-File = {Taxpayer-ID + Taxpayer-Name}

might well be approached by decomposing the design into modules, as shown in Figure 5.3. The result is that linkage code in the manager module can be written using the data-derived formulations presented above. In order to make this structure work, it is necessary for all modules to respect a read-ahead protocol on each input stream. (Wherever an input element is used, an immediate read must be instituted by the using module to stay one item ahead.) The read-ahead item enables the manager module to decide which module to invoke next.

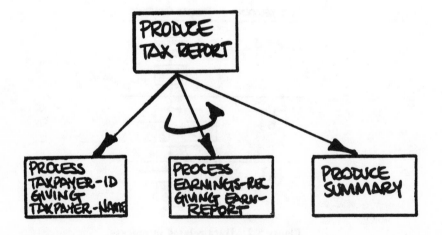

Figure 5.3: Data-derived structure.

## 5.4  Source Material on Data-Driven Design

The data-driven design approach has three main advocates: Warnier, Jackson, and Orr.  I cite one work by each.

Warnier's *Logical Construction of Programs* [WAR-1] is the classic.  This very early work makes an eloquent defense of micro application of data-driven design methods.

Jackson's *Principles of Program Design* [JAC-1] extends the concept substantially, and applies it at the macro level.  Jackson has developed a design methodology (only partially described in the cited book) to deal with complications introduced by badly meshing input and output structures as well as other practical problems.

Orr's *Structured Systems Development* [ORR-1] applies Warnier's thought process and graphics to an extended set of uses.  It updates and makes a clear presentation of Warnier's ideas.

# 6: information-hiding

Information-hiding is a design and coding discipline that calls for certain kinds of data to be concealed or "encapsulated" inside modules.

## 6.1 Principles of Information-Hiding

- Conceal complex data structures (stacks, pointer structures, arrays of strings, and so forth) whenever possible.

- Allow only selected service modules to know about the concealed data structure.

- Bind together modules that know about concealed data structures.

- Package such modules along with the data itself.

## 6.2 Rationale for Information-Hiding

Code readability is enhanced when high-level modules are spared any mention of complexities involved in handling awkward data structures. This is particularly true when awkwardness is the result of incompatability between the data and the language (for example, text strings and FORTRAN II or arithmetics and SNOBOL).

As a simple example, imagine a primitive language that has no array facilities but that does allow function calls. How might we arrange to deal with a required array? One solution would be to arrange some artificial representation of the array and then to allow all modules that access the array to know the representation. Information-hiding, on the other hand, would encourage us to package into one supermodule the representation and service routines that need to know about the representation. That supermodule then would simulate array facilities for all other modules.

Modern formal languages encourage information-hiding by blurring the distinction between data and process. For instance, the statement

DRAG = FORCE * SINE (THETA)

need not imply whether SINE is a subroutine that computes the sine as a function of THETA, or whether it is an array of sine values accessed by THETA. From the reader's point of view, the distinction usually is not relevant to understanding the module containing the statement. Which of the two implementations is used is purely a consideration of time versus space, a consideration that the reader decidedly should not have to grapple with at the upper levels.

## 6.3 Source Material on Information-Hiding

The concept of information-hiding usually is associated with the name Parnas. I cite here one rather theoretical work of his, as well as a book of design methods that describes practical applications of Parnas' work to everyday design problems:

Parnas' *On the Criteria to Be Used in Decomposing Systems into Modules* [PAR-4] sets out the principles of encapsulation and advocates a design methodology to minimize data visibility.

Myers' *Reliable Software Through Composite Design* [MYE-3] uses the idea of information-hiding as one of the criteria for evaluating strength of a module as well as for determining modular structure and interface characteristics.

# 7: pseudocode

The concept of pseudocoding modules as part of the detailed design phase came into fashion in the late 1960s. Most of the early experience was on projects in which the coding was to be written in assembly language. An appropriate higher-level language was invented to describe module structure and flow. The actual coding then consisted of translation of the pseudocode into assembly language instructions. Sometimes the pseudocode selected was PL/I or ALGOL or some other formal language. (In such cases, the translation could have been replaced by an esoteric computerized process called *compilation,* but this usually violated moral strictures of assembly language coders and was therefore seldom considered.)

More recently, there has been a trend toward pseudocoding certain modules, even though a higher-level language is to be used in coding.

## 7.1 Principles of Pseudocoding

☐ Adopt a high-level pseudocode that shows module invocations and passed parameters.

☐ Use this pseudocode to describe internal structure of any module in the hierarchy that manages other modules.

☐ Use the result as an early and relatively cheap gauge of the readability of resultant code.

☐ Pseudocode iteratively where code readability is poor, and/or consider changes to the hierarchy in order to eliminate internal problems.

## 7.2 Rationale for Pseudocoding

A common theme of software engineering is the idea that complex technical developments require an iterative approach. The human mind works efficiently at successive refinement of an idea; it is less efficient at coming up with perfection on the first try. Iterative coding can be burdensome because of the very exacting syntax of all formal languages. Pseudocoding allows the developer to experiment with many successive versions of a module with a minimum investment of time.

One of the major goals of any design technique is to assure readability of the code. But structural design treats modules as integral wholes (that is, it does not consider their "insides"). Pseudocoding is useful, in conjunction with structural design, to judge the effects of a given design decision on the readability of final code.

## 7.3 Conventions of Pseudocoding

The pseudocode convention* that I propose here is similar to Structured English. Like Structured English, it uses indentation as an integral part of the convention to show subordination. (There are no end-of-block markers in this pseudocode.) A necessary consequence of this approach is that no module can be so large as to require more than one page of pseudocode. The following additions to the Structured English are required for pseudocoding:

1.  Use capitalization, italics, or underlining to show module invocation. This avoids the problem of deciding what form of invocation will be used (CALL, PERFORM, DO, and so forth).

2.  Show passed parameters for each invocation in brackets. Separate downward-passing parameters from upward-passing parameters with a colon. Figure 7.1, shown on the following page, portrays a typical invocation written in pseudocode and the structure chart associated with it.

*For an example of pseudocode, see Figure 8.12.

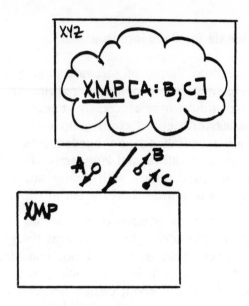

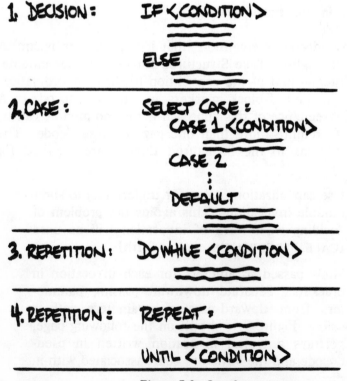

Figure 7.1: Structure chart and pseudocode invocation.

**1. DECISION:**   IF <CONDITION>

ELSE

**2. CASE:**   SELECT CASE :
   CASE 1 <CONDITION>

   CASE 2
   :
   DEFAULT

**3. REPETITION:**   DO WHILE <CONDITION>

**4. REPETITION:**   REPEAT :

UNTIL <CONDITION>

Figure 7.2: Legal constructs.

3.  Limit control structures to those portrayed in Figure 7.2, as shown on the previous page.

4.  When the convention fights you, abandon it: Write in plain-vanilla English, as in Figure 7.3, which is an example of relaxed pseudocode. (This example is adapted from material in [KER-3], a programming manual on the C language. The book is not about pseudocode, but it makes excellent use of the concept.)

WHILE (THERE'S ANOTHER LINE)
    IF (IT'S LONGER THAN PREVIOUS LONGEST)
        SAVE IT AND ITS LENGTH
PRINT THE LONGEST LINE

Figure 7.3:  Relaxed pseudocode.

## 7.4  Source Material on Pseudocode

The IPO portion of HIPO is something of a pseudocode. The convention is adequately described in [REF-3 and KAT-1]. The IPO approach suffers somewhat from its ill-conceived and overly restricted layouts. They make the pseudocoding process anything but iterative, since dealing with them is so time-consuming.

Since pseudocode is designed to give only an indication of readability while setting some guidelines for module internals, use of it requires a less-than-religious approach. What we do require is enough fluidity to make the process of writing pseudocode so rapid that designers will not hesitate to pseudocode a given module several times. A non-religious and well-thought-out approach to pseudocoding is provided by the following works:

Kernighan and Plauger [KER-1] advocate an outline form of pseudocode for drafting module internals. The book provides enough good examples to make the convention clear, although the authors never formally declare the convention itself. The implication is that each designer ought to be left free to develop his or her own particular approach.

Caine and Gordon [CAI-1] describe a pseudocoding convention called Program Design Language (PDL). PDL is quickly mastered and easy to write. The resultant pseudocode is clear enough for most users to be able to read. There is a software package available to check PDL syntax, but the convention is perfectly usable without the package (and perhaps more *useful,* since the package makes the language more restrictive than the designer might require).

Yourdon [YOU-4] presents a management-oriented book on implementing software development techniques. The book proposes a loose pseudocoding as an intermediate activity between Structured Design and coding. The convention is illustrated by example.

# 8: structured coding

The term "structured programming" has for many years been used to connote a discipline for part of the design task (detailed, or micro, design) together with a coding discipline. In *Concise Notes,* the term Structured Coding is used to refer to the coding discipline alone.

Structured Coding began during the late 1950s, with such names as Böhm and Jacopini, and Dijkstra, and Warnier. Such terms as "mainline programming," "goto-less coding," "top-down coding," and "straight-line coding" were used to describe the idea of building programs using limited control structures in order to enhance readability and ease of testing.

The discipline of Structured Coding owes its existence primarily to interest generated during the late 1950s and early 1960s in relation to the idea of program verification. In those days of extremely tight CPU-time, developers were concerned about the very large percentage of computer time spent in debugging. They argued the need for rigorous desk-checking procedures, called "proof of correctness algorithms."

At the time, in spite of much hand-waving on the subject, there were no algorithms for proving correctness. In fact, there wasn't even a coherent body of thought about what forms such algorithms should take. There was, however, a consensus that program simplicity was a good thing in general, and that simplicity of control structures would improve the likelihood of a program's ever being *proved* correct. Furthermore, program simplicity was deemed necessary if even some limited success were to be achieved in the field of program verification.

The clue to simplicity (and, hence, the hope of verification) seemed to be avoidance of some of the more esoteric logical formulations that many languages allowed. Clearly, there was no hope of ever proving correctness of a program that used the ALTER construct. So, in the interest of simplicity, that construct was abandoned. It was trivial to write programs without the ALTER. That realization set developers to wondering what else they could do without: What minimum subset of logical constructs would be sufficient to write all possible programs? Developers quickly came to the conclusion that they could live without the GOTO, SKIP, REMOTE EXECUTE, and a host of other constructs.

The minimal-construct sweepstakes finally were won by Böhm and Jacopini [BOH-3]. In their 1966 paper, a work whose importance to our field is exceeded only by its unreadability, they proved that only two logical formulations were necessary, showing that any program could be built up from two simple constructs (since called the Böhm and Jacopini constructs). Developers around the world began to try out Structured Coding, using these Böhm and Jacopini constructs.

In the ensuing twenty years, interest in proof of correctness has died out, largely because no one yet has been able to demonstrate a viable approach to proving the correctness of even the simplest program. But Structured Coding turned out to have numerous benefits other than that of assuring hope of eventual program verification. And so, the concept lived on beyond its original purposes.

## 8.1 Principles of Structured Coding

□ Write code with control (branching) formulations limited to the Böhm and Jacopini constructs (see Figure 8.1), plus the optional extensions shown in Figure 8.2.

□ Allow nesting (as in Figure 8.3).

□ Prohibit all other logical constructs. (Some of the disallowed constructs are shown in Figure 8.4.)

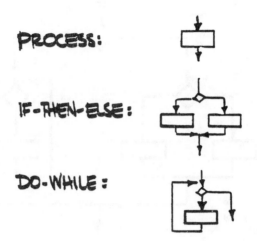

PROCESS:

IF-THEN-ELSE:

DO-WHILE:

Figure 8.1: Böhm and Jacopini constructs.

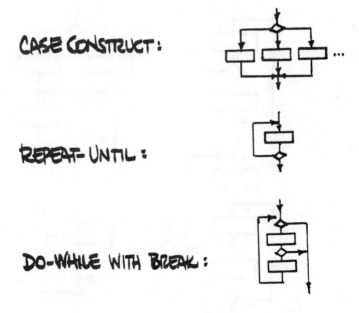

CASE CONSTRUCT:

REPEAT-UNTIL:

DO-WHILE WITH BREAK:

Figure 8.2: Extended constructs.

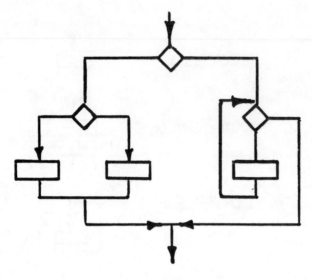

Figure 8.3: Nested constructs.

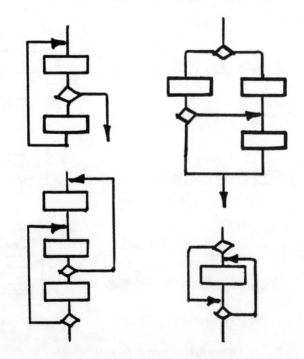

Figure 8.4: Disallowed constructs.

## 8.2  Rationale for Structured Coding

The rationale for Structured Coding is, of course, that its use reduces life-time system cost. It has been shown to increase productivity, and, in particular, to reduce the manpower required for testing and integration [MIL-2 and YOU-2].

In order to understand why Structured Coding has these marvelous effects, consider the unstructured flowchart of Figure 8.5. Look at it very carefully. The flowchart is simple enough, and you might suspect that its use could not lead to great complications. However, that judgment is premature. So far you have only *looked at* the logic involved — that is, you have used the picture-processing portion of your mind to absorb the figure's content. Unfortunately, the logic must next be reduced to code, a one-dimensional medium. From that point on, the logic cannot be looked at. As code, it must be *read,* using one of the brain's one-dimensional facilities. But the logic involved is intrinsically two-dimensional, and thus will always be difficult to read.

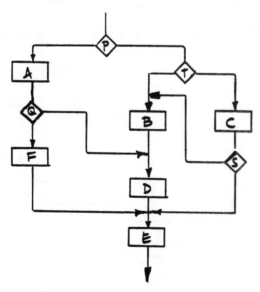

**Figure 8.5:  Unstructured flowchart.**

Readability is enhanced by reformulating the logic to make it more nearly one-dimensional. (See Figure 8.6, which represents a *serialized* version of the same logic.) The flowchart in Figure 8.6 is not particularly simpler to understand than Figure 8.5, but the resultant code is. Because it proceeds smoothly from top to bottom, using only the single-entry, single-exit constructs, it is more easily digested by the brain's one-dimensional reading center.

The concept of linearizing code in order to enhance readability is the rationale behind Structured Coding.

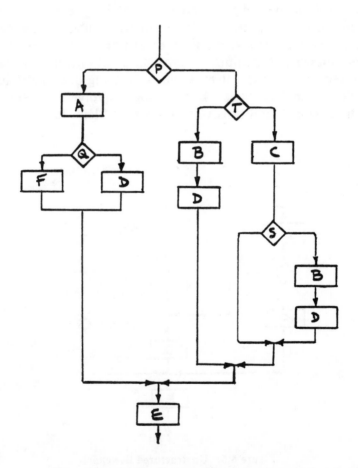

**Figure 8.6: Structured equivalent of Figure 8.5.**

## 8.3  Conventions of Structured Coding

Presented below is an extended set of Structured Coding constructs and a pseudocode implementation for each one. The equivalent implementation in any given language should be straightforward. Note, however, that if the target language is primitive (FORTRAN, BASIC, APL, and so on), it may not be possible to completely avoid the use of the GOTO. Disciplined use of GOTOs to implement legitimate structured constructs is entirely consistent with good Structured Coding in such languages.

### The IF-ELSE Construct

IF  <condition>
    <code to be executed
    if condition is true>
ELSE
    <code to be executed
    if condition not true>

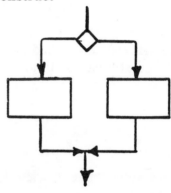

Figure 8.7:  IF-ELSE construct.

### The DO-WHILE Construct

DO-WHILE  <condition>
    <repeated code>

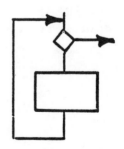

Figure 8.8:  DO-WHILE construct.

## The REPEAT-UNTIL Construct

REPEAT
    <repeated code>
UNTIL <condition>

Figure 8.9: REPEAT-UNTIL construct.

Note that code embodied in the REPEAT-UNTIL construct always is executed at least one time.

## DO-WHILE with Break

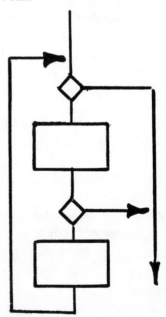

DO-WHILE <condition>
    <repeated code>
    IF <break condition>
        BREAK
    <extension of repeated code>

Figure 8.10: DO-WHILE with break.

## The CASE Construct

CASE OF <case variable(s)>

    CASE 1: <condition defining case 1>
            <code to be executed if case 1>
    CASE 2: <condition defining case 2>
            <code to be executed if case 2>
    CASE 3: <condition defining case 3>
    .
    .

    .
    DEFAULT:
            <code to be executed if default>

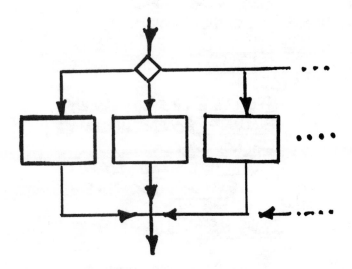

Figure 8.11: CASE construct.

Of course, it is permissible to combine and nest legal constructs. Figure 8.12, shown on the following page, is a pseudocode example that makes use of several different constructs in nested fashion.

```
REPEAT:
     QUERY PLAYER ["ELECT BLACK OR WHITE": RESPONSE]
     CASE OF RESPONSE:
          CASE 1: RESPONSE = "BLACK" OR "B"
                 INITIALIZE-BOARD ["BLACK": BOARD]
                 MOVE [BOARD: BOARD]
          CASE 2: RESPONSE = "WHITE" OR "W"
                 INITIALIZE-BOARD ["WHITE": BOARD]
          DEFAULT:
                 ISSUE-MSG ["TRY AGAIN"]
UNTIL (BOARD INITIALIZED)
EVALUATE [BOARD : CHECKMATE]
DO-WHILE (NOT CHECKMATE)
     QUERY-PLAYER [" MOVE? " : RESPONSE]
     EDIT RESPONSE [RESPONSE: MOVE, OK]
     IF (OK)
          APPLY [MOVE , BOARD: BOARD]
          EVALUATE [BOARD: CHECKMATE]
          IF (NOT CHECKMATE)
                MOVE [BOARD : BOARD]
                EVALUATE [BOARD: CHECKMATE]
     ELSE
          ISSUE MSG ["ILLEGAL MOVE"]
```

Figure 8.12:  Combined constructs.

## 8.4  Source Material on Structured Coding

The original source material on Structured Coding is fragmented and largely theoretical. I confine mention here to the more practical how-to publications:

Yourdon's *Techniques of Program Structure and Design* [YOU-2] presents the method, meaning, and justification for Structured Coding. It is useful as a single, complete reference on the subject.

Language-oriented Structured Coding texts and manuals [MCC-3, YOU-8, LIS-1, KER-3, GEL-1, WEI-3] offer specific implementations of the limited constructs in each target language. As such, they can present the concept in terms that are particularly germane to coders.

Weinberg's *High Level COBOL Programming* [WEI-5] also is language-specific (COBOL), but it takes rather a different tack: It encourages the use of a preprocessor to cope with special obstructions that COBOL throws up against the structured coder.

Kernighan and Plauger's *Software Tools* [KER-2] does for FORTRAN what [WEI-5] does for COBOL, that is, it advocates use of a preprocessor (RATFOR) to allow structuring of FORTRAN.

For those interested in the original works on Structured Coding, Ed Yourdon's *Classics in Software Engineering* [YOU-6] presents a collection of significant papers published over the past 15 years. The book includes the editor's comments on the impact of each work.

# 9: top-down implementation

Top-down implementation is a testing and integration discipline. It is used as an alternative to the more classical "phased" implementation. Phased implementation consists of the following successive activities:

- coding
- unit-testing
- subsystem assembly and testing
- system and integration testing

Phased integration is weak in that key interfaces are not tested until the very end, when subsystems are interconnected. Major hypotheses remain in doubt until the very end. The most important portions of the system are exercised least. The result can be a project that remains stuck at 95 percent completed for 50 percent of the time.

## 9.1 Principles of Top-Down Implementation

☐ Assemble the top of the structure first.

☐ Replace missing subordinates by stub test-modules.

☐ Implement successive layers from the top.

☐ Select versions (assemblies) in such a way as to show increasing amounts of critical system function.

## 9.2 Definitions of Top-Down Implementation Terms

A STUB is a test routine that drives a module from beneath. Viewed from above, the stub has the same characteristics (name and calling sequence) as the simulated module. A stub may consist of the following elements:

- an immediate return
- return passing back a fixed test value
- debugging snapshots
- general-purpose stub that solicits guidance from a terminal as to what to return
- performance simulating delay

A VERSION is a layer of modules assembled with stubs replacing not-yet-implemented subordinates.

## 9.3 Rationale for Top-Down Implementation

The advantages of top-down implementation fall into these categories:

- improved quality of the product due to added exercise of the more important upper levels
- reduced risk due to early verification of key hypotheses (including some indication of performance)
- improved political situation due to early visibility of partial products

As an example, consider the system represented at the top of the next page in Figure 9.1, which shows a multi-tasking application implemented with co-routines.

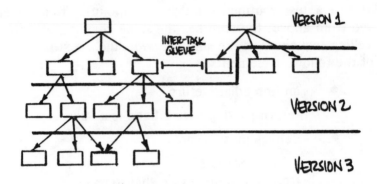

**Figure 9.1: Versioned implementation.**

The very first version depicted in Figure 9.1 begins to exercise the critical intertask interface. The second version actually accepts live input and produces one of the real outputs, shown further in Version 3.

For most systems, only a minor proportion of delivered code is concerned with what users think of as the system's function. Most of the code deals with exceptions. It is quite normal for ten percent of the code to do ninety percent of the system's required work, and for fifty percent of the code to deal with situations that (taken all together) occur only one percent of the time. To the extent that early versions can be cleverly selected, they provide surprisingly realistic simulations of the real system.

## 9.4 Source Material on Top-Down Implementation

The original source on top-down implementation is the IBM New York Times project. Three papers reporting on that project were prepared by F.T. Baker, in one case in collaboration with H.D. Mills [BAK-1, BAK-2, and BAK-3]. All three papers are reprinted in [YOU-6].

# 10: software metrics

The term "software metrics" refers to the measurement of quantitative indicators of a system's size and complexity. Such indicators then are used to correlate against past observed performance in order to derive predictions of future performance.

The discipline of software metrics received a great deal of attention in the early years of our industry, but was nearly abandoned around 1960. The reason for disenchantment was a general inability to hit upon usable predictive indicators when performance seemed to fluctuate so wildly and be subject to so many controlling factors.

In recent years, the concept has become popular again, although today's adherents have discarded the simplistic approaches of the past. Predictive derivations today are seen to depend on literally dozens of factors.

## 10.1 Principles of Software Metrics

☐ Specialize the estimating and performance data-collection functions.

☐ Assign these responsibilities for all projects to a special-purpose team.

☐ Collect performance data pertaining to software delivery.

☐ Express results in terms of net lines of executable code (NLOEC) delivered.

☐ Observe Walston-Felix factors (or equivalent) for each project, and compile these together with performance and size data into project history records.

□ Analyze past project histories to determine the effect of these factors.

□ Use these effects to weight future predictions.

□ Estimate by using early quantum indicators (number of functional primitives and data elements) to predict NLOEC.

□ Use predicted NLOEC and predicted W-F factor to derive base estimates for new development.

□ Vary from derived base estimate to take account of factors not figured in the formula.

## 10.2 Definitions of Software Metrics Terms

The WALSTON-FELIX FACTORS are a set of parameters known to affect productivity. (See the Appendix for a partial list of the actual factors.)

NET LINES OF EXECUTABLE CODE is the count of delivered source language statements in a module minus comment lines, data declarations, and pseudo-operators (compiler listing commands, START, END, and so on). Macro-defining lines are to be counted once only (not for each call). Each macro call counts as one line. Test drivers, stubs, and test data generators are not counted.

## 10.3 Rationale for Software Metrics

Measurement of the emerging product is essential for

- predicting the rest of the project
- judging progress
- judging (and reducing) complexity

Without some means of quantitative assessment, management is obliged to take it on faith alone that progress is being made, and that the rate of progress is satisfactory.

Through specialization of the estimating function (as well as data collection for future estimates), we can hope to build estimating expertise. Under this scheme, responsibility for all estimating in an organization is centralized. A single team of estimators quantifies all projects, predicts development time and effort, and tracks the project through its completion. Advantages of this approach are

- estimators have no emotional stake in the project (a factor that is known to cloud judgment)

- estimators can be made relatively free from pressures to come up with "the right answer"

- estimators have the incentive to improve the quality of their estimates by collecting relevant correlative data

- estimators can hope to learn through substantial repetition

- centrally controlled data collection will result in homogeneous measurement

## 10.4 Conventions of Software Metrics

No software metrics techniques can be of use in predicting future performance until a significant sampling of past project histories has been assembled. Historical data must be collected according to a rigorous standard. Data collected about each project should include:

- NLOEC
- work-hours to deliver by activity
- staff size as a function of phase
- elapsed time by phase
- cost

In addition, factors affecting project efficiency should be collected. A useful set of such factors has been compiled by Walston and Felix [WAL-1] in empirical studies at IBM.

In place of abstract recommendations about project tracking and data collection, I have included in the Appendix the specific standard and all relevant forms and reports used to track projects in the 1978 and 1979 YOURDON Project Surveys. A reduced list of the Walston-Felix factors also is included in the Appendix.

Once a sample of past projects has been compiled, future estimates can be geared to it. A predictive formula is derived by expressing past delivery results per NLOEC, and weighting the estimates by each of the factors. Note that some estimating remains to be performed (What, for example, is the weighting factor of a new language or test vehicle?), but that only *deviations* are estimated. The base prediction is derived.

Effectiveness of this technique requires that past estimating errors result in modifications to derivation formulas.

For estimates required prior to empirical count of NLOEC, the following indicators may be used:

- During analysis, use a count of functional primitives and/or data elements in the specification model in order to predict NLOEC (using past observed relationships).
- During design, use a count of modules correlated back to past NLOEC per module.

Of course, tolerance to be applied to each prediction is a function of how early the prediction is made. Tolerances should be derived from past estimate errors.

## 10.5 Metrics of Code Complexity

Measurable indications of code complexity can be used to reduce complexity as well as to predict development time. Commonly used complexity metrics follow:

- count of decisions [MCC-1, GIL-1]
- count of "knots" [WOO-1] (A knot is an intersection of control paths linking come-from points to go-to points.)

## 10.6  Source Material on Software Metrics

Walston and Felix's *A Method of Programming Measurement and Estimation* [WAL-1] is an excellent treatment of the subject. It provides measurement techniques and observed data from a large sample of projects at IBM.

Halstead's *Elements of Software Science* [HAL-1] is theoretical in nature.  It develops complexity measures and predictive formulas in great detail.

# appendix

## YOURDON PROJECT SURVEY
## DATA COLLECTION STANDARD

Project-tracking data collection involves the following four kinds of reports:

*Initial Report:* Consists of a questionnaire and project abstract. This report should be filed once, at the beginning of the survey.

*Monthly Progress Report:* Indicates time billed against the project in each of several categories. This report should be filed at the beginning of each month, reporting time accounted against the project during the previous month. If your project already has started at the time of your Initial Report, an initial Progress Report should be filed that documents the time previously billed against the project.

*End of Project Report:* Details characteristics of the delivered work. This report should be filed when the project is completed or otherwise terminated.

*Follow-up Report:* Indicates experience with the delivered system in the production environment. This report should be filed six months after completion of the project.

The reports are described more fully in the following sections. Prototype reports are appended to this document.

### 1. The Initial Report

The Initial Report establishes a profile for the project. It assigns a project name, describes the project briefly, and then fills in known parameters that may be expected to affect performance. The Initial Report consists of a completed Project Profile Questionnaire and a one-page project abstract.

Many of the questions in the Project Profile Questionnaire are based on Walston and Felix's paper [WAL-1], published in the January 1977 *IBM Systems Journal.*

The abstracts will be entered verbatim into the project record and distributed at the end of the survey as part of the final report. For this reason, please make certain that no information in the abstract is company-confidential. Make sure that the abstract does not give away your company's identity, and select a project name that will maintain your company's confidentiality. We guarantee that your participation will not be made public in any of the rest of the published results, but the "sanitizing" of the abstract is up to you.

The business of measuring project parameters is so complex that no one yet qualifies as a true expert. Certainly I do not. I may have omitted questions from the profile that have an essential bearing on the final result. If you become aware of such an omission, please call it to my attention. Comments about any additional characteristics of your project that seem likely to be important should be inserted into the Miscellaneous Parameters Section of the profile. I look to you as the final judge of what data must be collected about your project.

## 2. The Progress Report

The Progress Report is a record of personnel time billed against the project during the reporting period. All personnel time is measured in *work-hours*. Target precision is plus or minus five percent.

For the purposes of this survey, time is billed against the project in these categories:

- *Analysis:* time spent determining WHAT the system will do. Included in Analysis are such activities as user interface, specification, modeling, functional design (determination of features to be implemented), feasibility study, cost-benefit analysis, and user procedures analysis.

- *Design:* determination of HOW the system will effect its required functions. Included in Design, as the term is used here, are determination of modular structure, intermodular interface design, data design, design documentation, and packaging.

- *Hardware Study:* including hardware selection, evaluation of impact on current configuration, benchmarking, and so forth.

- *Coding:* including all source code, comments, data declarations, macro definitions and calls, JCL, and test routines.

- *Testing:* including test plan preparation, test design, test data generation, test execution, and documentation. For the purposes of this survey, all tests from unit testing through acceptance testing are included in this single category.

- *Methods:* time spent developing project standards, test tools, techniques, and so on.

- *Conversion and Conversion Planning:* preparation for post-development system operation, including cutover, forms and procedures design, planning for parallel operation, and data conversion.

- *User Training:* including writing of user manuals, actual training sessions, support.

- *Review:* time spent in walkthroughs and other forms of peer product review.

- *Contract Administration:* preparation of Requests for Proposal, vendor selection, and monitoring.

- *Management:* all time spent directing the participation of others, reporting on the project, arranging personnel interfaces, and teams. Only direct project management should be included; no overhead.

- *Other:* direct project manpower not covered under any other category.

For purposes of consistency, no user participation should be recorded. Clerical support (keypunch, secretarial, librarian) should not be recorded, nor should machine operator time.

Vacation, sick time, and personal time-off should not be recorded.

Each Progress Report will consist of a one-page table of allocated time. (A prototype form is included at the end of this document.) Time is measured in work-hours. Each report should cover a calendar month, rounded to include integral weeks. Time statistics should be collected on a weekly basis. (Collecting data monthly on how each hour was spent would be sure to encourage precision that exceeded accuracy.)

A section is provided on the form to record changes in project manpower. Notes on relevant changes in project status should be included on the back of the form. Particularly important to cover in the Notes section are any changes to the profile parameters presented in the Initial Report.

## 3. The End of Project Report

The end of the project is marked by termination of all coding and testing and by acceptance of the system by user staff. At this time, a report should be filed to characterize the product delivered. The End of Project Report consists of a completed Product Questionnaire (prototype appended).

## 4. The Follow-up Report

Six months after the end of the project, a Follow-up Report should be filed. This report will consist of a completed Follow-up Questionnaire (see prototype).

In order to complete the last report, it will be necessary to keep an experience log during the six months following user acceptance. The log should record instances of system failure, occurrence of user-requested changes, and the manpower required to service and modify the system. It also should keep track of total system use (runs, hours, cycles).

# PROJECT PROFILE QUESTIONNAIRE

To the best of your ability, answer each of the following questions about your project. Where an estimate is called for, try to come up with an estimate that you think is equally likely to be high as low. When the question makes no sense to you or clearly does not apply to your project, leave the answer blank.

## A. Project Identification

1. Project name:

2. Company name (will be deleted from record):

3. Project start date:

4. Estimated completion date:

## B. Scope of Development

5. Total estimated manpower in work-hours:

6. Initial staff count:

7. Maximum staff count:

8. Number of managerial personnel assigned to project:

9. Estimated project duration in months:

10. Count of users expected to participate in project:

11. On-line or batch:

12. Interface to other automated systems:

13. New hardware to be used for development:

14. New operating system to be used for development:

15. Is the project a modification of an existing system:

16. Does this qualify more nearly as an "application" or "system" project:

17. Will the program or system produced be offered for sale as a package:

18. Is the product an operating system or part of one:

19. Estimate the maximum number of direct users of the product:

20. What percent of his/her work-time will the average staff member dedicate to the project:

21. How many hours make up the official work-week for project personnel:

22. Are personnel paid overtime for time worked beyond official hours:

## C. Development Environment

23. Do you intend to use Structured Analysis?

24. Do you intend to write a formal specification to document requirements?

25. Do you intend to use Structured Design or any variant thereof?

26. Do you intend to use Structured Coding?

27. Do you intend to do a top-down implementation?

28. Will the project have a librarian available to supply clerical support?

29. Is a text editing system available for documentation?

30. Will debugging be interactive?

31. What programming language will be used?

32. If assembly language, will macros be used extensively?

33. Will walkthroughs be used during analysis?

34. During design?

35.  During coding?

36.  Will you use the Chief Programmer Team approach?

37.  What other programmer productivity techniques will you make use of?

38.  Will development be subcontracted?

39.  Will the product be subject to formal acceptance testing procedures?

## D. Walston-Felix Factors

In the January 1977 *IBM Systems Journal,* Walston and Felix identified the following factors as useful in calculating a complexity index for development. Estimate each of the factors for your project by circling one of the answers provided.

40.  Customer (user) interface complexity:

Simple              Normal              Complex

41.  User participation in definition of requirements:

None              Some              Much

42.  Customer (user) originated program design changes:

Few                                   Many

43.  Customer (user) experience with the application area of project:

None              Some              Much

44.  Overall personnel experience and qualifications:

Low              Average              High

45.  Percentage of programmers who will have participated in the analysis and design:

Under 25%        25–50%              Over 50%

46. Previous experience with operational computer:

   Minimal            Average            Extensive

47. Previous experience with programming language to be used:

   Minimal            Average            Extensive

48. Previous experience with application of similar or greater size and complexity:

   Minimal            Average            Extensive

49. Ratio of average staff size to duration (people/month):

   Less than .5        .5−.9              Greater than .9

50. Hardware under concurrent development:

   No                 Yes

51. Development computer access, open under special request:

   0%                 1−25%              Greater than 25%

52. Development computer access, closed:

   0−10%              11−85%             Greater than 85%

53. Classified security environment for computer and at least 25% of programs and data:

   No                 Yes

54. Use of Structured Programming (expressed as a percentage of code written using only the control constructs SEQUENCE, DO-UNTIL or WHILE, IF-THEN-ELSE, and CASE):

   0−33%              34−66%             Greater than 66%

55. Percent of all design and code subject to a formal walk-through:

   0−33%              34−66%             Greater than 66%

56. Use of top-down development (expressed as a percent adherence to the concept of designing, coding, and testing calling modules before their called modules):

   0–33%              34–66%              Greater than 66%

57. Use of the concept of the Chief Programmer Team:

   None               Partial              Rigorous

58. Overall complexity of code delivered:

   Less than average   Average             Greater than average

59. Complexity of application processing:

   Less than average   Average             Greater than average

60. Complexity of program flow:

   Less than average   Average             Greater than average

61. Overall constraints on program design:

   Minimal            Average              Severe

62. Program design constraints on main storage:

   Minimal            Average              Severe

63. Program design constraints on timing:

   Minimal            Average              Severe

64. Code for real-time or interactive operation, or executing under severe timing constraint:

   Less than 10%      10–40%               Greater than 40%

65. Percentage of code for delivery:

   0–90%              91–99%               100%

66. Code classified as non-mathematical applications and I/O formatting programs:

   0–33%              34–66%               67–100%

67. Number of classes of items in the database per 1000 lines of code:

   0–15             16–80             80+

68. Number of pages of delivered documentation per 1000 lines of delivered code:

   0–32             33–88             88+

## E. Miscellaneous Parameters

69. What other characteristics of your project are (in your opinion) likely to have a strong effect on ultimate productivity?

## F. Initial Estimates

Give your best estimate of source lines of code that will be delivered in each of the following categories:

70. JCL:

71. Executable statements:

72. Data declarations:

73. Comments:

74. Other:

75. Total:

## G. Project Abstract

Write a one-page project abstract to describe your project. Include details that seem relevant and unique. Describe the product to be delivered as well as the project itself. Attach your abstract to this completed questionnaire.

## MONTHLY PROGRESS REPORT

Company: _____ Project: _____

Reporting Period: From: _____ Until: _____

### Time Charged Against Project

During this period, the following time (work-hours) was charged against the project by category:

- Analysis:
- Design:
- Hardware Study:
- Coding:
- Testing:
- Methods:
- Conversion and Conversion Planning:
- User Training:
- Review:
- Contract Administration:
- Management:
- Other (specify):
- Total:

**Current Project Structure**

The current project staff count is   _____.

Of this number, the count of managerial personnel is

_____.

Percent of total work-time dedicated to this project for the average staff member is   _____.

**Notes**

Record below any significant changes in the project since the last report.   Include, in particular, any changes of those project characteristics recorded in the initial Project Profile.

# END OF PROJECT REPORT

Company: _____  Project: _____

Project end date: _____

Answer the following questions about your project to the best of your ability. If the question makes no sense to you or is clearly not applicable to your project, leave the answer blank.

## A. Project Status at End

1. Did the project run to normal completion?

2. Was it cancelled before completion?

3. Was it suspended with a view toward later completion?

4. Was the product accepted by user staff?

5. Is the product now in use?

6. If there was a formal acceptance test, did it run successfully on the first try?

7. Was the documentation of requirement still up to date as of the end of the project?

8. What staff has been allocated to maintenance of the product?

## B.  Product Description

Describe the delivered program or system quantitatively by answering the following questions. Try to answer within five percent accuracy. Where it is necessary to estimate, form estimate from extrapolation of a sample portion of the product.

All lines of code (LOC) counts refer to source language lines. Counts of delivered pages of documentation should be exclusive of program listings.

9.  How many LOC of JCL were delivered?

10.  How many LOC of executable code were delivered?

11.  How many LOC of data declarations were delivered?

12.  How many LOC of comments were delivered?

13.  How many LOC were delivered that did not fit into any of the four preceding categories?

14.  How many total LOC were delivered (sum of five preceding items)?

15.  How many additional LOC were written but not delivered (test routines, test data, and so forth)?

16.  What percentage of delivered LOC of executable statements were decisions? (A decision is any source line that involves conditional transfer of control: for example, IF, PERFORM UNTIL, DO-WHILE, CASE, BNE, BCTL.)

17.  What percentage of delivered LOC of executable statements were subroutine calls of some form (CALL, PERFORM, BAL)? Do not count those PERFORMs in COBOL whose use is principally for looping.

18.  How many unconditional GOTOs were included in delivered code?

19.  If assembly language was used, what percentage of all source statements were macro calls?

20. How many pages of documentation were delivered?

21. Of the total, how many pages document requirements?

22. How many pages document the design?

23. How many pages document code?

24. How many pages document use of the system?

25. How many pages of all other documentation?

26. Was the specification of requirements ever formally frozen?

27. If so, at what point?

## C. Revision of Estimated Factors

As part of the initial Project Profile, you were asked to estimate certain factors (called the Walston-Felix factors) expected to have a strong effect on productivity. Please reevaluate these factors now, stating actual results for your project. Answer each question by circling the most accurate of the answers provided.

28. Customer (user) interface complexity:

   Simple          Normal          Complex

29. User participation in definition of requirements:

   None            Some            Much

30. Customer (user) originated program design changes:

   Few                             Many

31. Customer (user) experience with the application area of project:

   None            Some            Much

32. Overall personnel experience and qualifications:

   Low             Average         High

33. Percentage of programmers who participated in the analysis and design:

   Under 25%          25−50%          Over 50%

34. Previous experience with operational computer:

   Minimal          Average          Extensive

35. Previous experience with programming language used:

   Minimal          Average          Extensive

36. Previous experience with application of similar or greater size and complexity:

   Minimal          Average          Extensive

37. Ratio of average staff size to duration (people/month):

   Less than .5          .5−.9          Greater than .9

38. Hardware under concurrent development:

   No          Yes

39. Development computer access, open under special request:

   0%          1−25%          Greater than 25%

40. Development computer access, closed:

   0−10%          11−85%          Greater than 85%

41. Classified security environment for computer and for at least 25% of programs and data:

   No          Yes

42. Use of Structured Programming (expressed as a percentage of code written using only the control constructs SEQUENCE, DO-UNTIL or WHILE, IF-THEN-ELSE, and CASE):

   0−33%          34−66%          Greater than 66%

43. Percent of all design and code subject to a formal walk-through:

    0–33%                34–66%                Greater than 66%

44. Use of top-down development (expressed as a percent adherence to the concept of designing, coding, and testing calling modules before their called modules):

    0–33%                34–66%                Greater than 66%

45. Use of the concept of the Chief Programmer Team:

    None                Partial                Rigorous

46. Overall complexity of code delivered:

    Less than average    Average                Greater than average

47. Complexity of application processing:

    Less than average    Average                Greater than average

48. Complexity of program flow:

    Less than average    Average                Greater than average

49. Overall constraints on program design:

    Minimal              Average                Severe

50. Program design constraints on main storage:

    Minimal              Average                Severe

51. Program design constraints on timing:

    Minimal              Average                Severe

52. Code for real-time or interactive operation, or executing under severe timing constraint:

    Less than 10%        10–40%                 Greater than 40%

53. Percentage of code for delivery:

    0–90%                91–99%                 100%

54. Code classified as non-mathematical applications and I/O formatting programs:

    0–33%              34–66%              67–100%

55. Number of classes of items in the database per 1000 lines of code:

    0–15               16–80               80+

56. Number of pages of delivered documentation per 1000 lines of delivered code:

    0–32               33–88               88+

## D. Miscellaneous Parameters

57. What other parameters affected productivity, in your opinion?

# FOLLOW-UP REPORT

Company: _____    Project: _____

Project end date: _____

Date of this report: _____

Answer the following questions from the observed pattern of maintenance required and requested for your delivered program or system:

1. How many unique bugs have been detected?

2. How many of these have been fixed?

3. How many new or revised lines of source code (JCL, executable, data, and comments) were required on the average for each fix?

4. How much manpower (average) has been required per fix?

5. How many changes and enhancements have been requested since installation of the system?

6. How many of these have been put in?

7. How many lines of source code (JCL, executable, data, and comments) were required on the average for each change?

8. How many bugs were noted in the first month after delivery?

9. In the second month?

10. In the third month?

11. In the fourth month?

12. In the fifth month?

13. In the sixth month?

14. How many user change requests were received in the first month after delivery?

15. In the second month?

16. In the third month?

17. In the fourth month?

18. In the fifth month?

19. In the sixth month?

20. What manpower is presently allocated to maintenance of the product?

21. How much total effort (in work-hours) has been spent on the project since delivery?

# bibliography

ALE-1    Alexander, C. *Notes on the Synthesis of Form.* Cambridge, Mass.: Harvard University Press, 1977.

AMM-1    Ammann, U. "The Method of Structured Programming Applied to the Development of a Compiler." *Proceedings of the 1973 International Computing Symposium.* Amsterdam, The Netherlands: North-Holland Publishing Co., 1974, pp. 93-100.

ARO-1    Aron, J. "The Super-Programmer Project." *Software Engineering, Concepts and Techniques,* eds. J.M. Buxton, P. Naur, and B. Randell. New York: Petrocelli/Charter, 1976, pp. 188-90. (See also [YOU-6].)

ASH-1    Ashcroft, E., and Z. Manna. "The Translation of 'go to' Programs to 'while' Programs." *Proceedings of the 1971 IFIP Congress,* Vol. I. Amsterdam, The Netherlands: North-Holland Publishing Co., 1972, pp. 250-55. (See also [YOU-6].)

ASS-1    Asser, G. "Functional Algorithms and Graph Schema." *Z. Math. Logik u. Grundlagen Math.,* Vol. 7 (1961), pp. 20-27.

BAK-1    Baker, F.T. "Chief Programmer Team Management of Production Programming." *IBM Systems Journal,* Vol. 11, No. 1 (January 1972), pp. 56-73. (See also [YOU-6].)

BAK-2    _____. "System Quality Through Structured Programming." *AFIPS Proceedings of the 1972 Fall Joint Computer Conference,* Vol. 41, Part I. Montvale, N.J.: AFIPS Press, 1972, pp. 339-44. (See also [YOU-6].)

BAK-3    _____, and H.D. Mills. "Chief Programmer Teams." *Datamation,* Vol. 19, No. 12 (December 1973), pp. 58-61. (See also [YOU-6].)

81

BAL-1    Balbine, G. "Better Manpower Utilization Using Automatic Restructuring." *AFIPS Proceedings of the 1975 National Computer Conference,* Vol. 44, Part I. Montvale, N.J.: AFIPS Press, 1975, pp. 319-34.

BAL-2    Balzer, R.M. "Dataless Programming." *Proceedings of the 1967 AFIPS Fall Joint Computer Conference,* Vol. 31. Montvale, N.J.: AFIPS Press, 1967, pp. 535-44.

BEL-2    Belady, L.A., and M.M. Lehman. *Programming System Dynamics or the Metadynamics of Systems in Maintenance and Growth.* IBM Corp., RC 3546. Yorktown Heights, N.Y.: IBM Thomas J. Watson Research Center, 1971.

BOE-1    Boehm, B.W. "Software Engineering." *IEEE Transactions on Computers,* Vol. C-25, No. 12 (December 1976), pp. 1226-41. (See also [YOU-6].)

BOH-1    Böhm, C. "On a Family of Turing Machines and the Related Programming Language," *ICC Bulletin,* Vol. 3 (July 1964), pp. 187-94.

BOH-2    _____, and G. Jacopini. "Nuove Tecniche di Programmazione Semplificanti la Sintesi di Macchine Universali di Turing." *Rend. Acc. Naz. Lincei,* Vol. 8, No. 32 (June 1962), pp. 913-22.

BOH-3    _____. "Flow Diagrams, Turing Machines and Languages with Only Two Formation Rules." *Communications of the ACM,* Vol. 9, No. 5 (May 1966), pp. 366-71. (See also [YOU-6].)

BRO-1    Brooks, F.P., Jr. *The Mythical Man-Month.* Reading, Mass.: Addison-Wesley, 1975.

BRU-1    Bruno, J., and K. Steiglitz. "The Expression of Algorithms by Charts." *Journal of the ACM,* Vol. 19, No. 3 (July 1972), pp. 517-25.

BUR-1    Burstall, R. "An Algebraic Description of Programs with Assertions, Verification and Simulation." *Proceedings of the ACM Conference on Proving Assertions About Programs, SIGPLAN Notices,* Vol. 7, No. 1 (January 1972), pp. 7-14.

CAI-1    Caine, S.H., and E.K. Gordon. "PDL — A Tool for Software Design." *AFIPS Proceedings of the 1975 National Computer Conference,* Vol. 44, Part I. Montvale, N.J.: AFIPS Press, 1975, pp. 271-76.

CAM-1    Campos, I.M., and G. Estrin. "Concurrent Software System Design Supported by SARA at the Age of One." *Third International Conference on Software Engineering,* IEEE Catalog No. 78CH1317-7C. New York: IEEE, 1978, pp. 230-42.

CIA-1    Ciampa, S. "Un'applicazione della Teoria dei Grafi." *Atti del Convegno Nazionale di Logica,* Vol. 5, No. 7 (Turin: April 1961), pp. 73-80.

CON-1    Conrow, K., and R.G. Smith. "NEATER2: A PL/I Source Statement Reformatter." *Communications of the ACM,* Vol. 13, No. 11 (November 1970), pp. 669-75.

CON-2    Constantine, L.L. "Control of Sequence and Parallelism in Modular Programs." *Proceedings of the 1968 AFIPS Spring Joint Computer Conference,* Vol. 32 (1968), p. 409.

COO-1    Cooper, D.C. "Böhm and Jacopini's Reduction of Flowcharts." *Communications of the ACM,* Vol. 10, No. 8 (August 1967), pp. 463-73.

COU-1    Couger, J.D. "Evolution of Business System Analysis Techniques." *ACM Computing Surveys,* Vol. 5, No. 3 (September 1973), pp. 167-98.

DAH-1    Dahl, O.J., E.W. Dijkstra, and C.A.R. Hoare. *Structured Programming.* New York: Academic Press, 1972.

DEL-1    *Structured Design.* Videotape series. Chicago: DEL-TAK inc.

DEL-2    *Structured Analysis.* Videotape series. Chicago: DEL-TAK inc.

DEM-1    DeMarco, T. "Report on the 1977 Productivity Survey." YOURDON inc., September 1977.

DEM-2 ———. "Breaking the Language Barrier." *Compu-terworld,* Vol. 12, Nos. 32, 33, and 34 (August 7, 14, and 21, 1978). Published in parts.

DEM-3 ———. *Structured Analysis and System Specification.* New York: YOURDON Press, 1978.

DEM-4 ———. "Structured Analysis and System Specification." *Proceedings of the GUIDE 47 Conference.* Chicago: GUIDE International Corp., 1978. (See also [YOU-6].)

DIJ-1 Dijkstra, E.W. "Go To Statement Considered Harmful." *Communications of the ACM,* Vol. 11, No. 3 (March 1968), pp. 147-48. (See also [YOU-6].)

DIJ-2 ———. "A Constructive Approach to the Problem of Program Correctness." *BIT,* Vol. 8, No. 3 (1968), pp. 174-86.

DIJ-3 ———. "The Structure of the 'THE'-Multiprogramming System," *Communications of the ACM,* Vol. 11, No. 5 (May 1968), 341-46.

DIJ-4 ———. *Notes on Structured Programming,* 2nd ed. Technische Hogeschool Eindhoven, Report No. EWD-248, 70-WSK-0349. Eindhoven, The Netherlands: April 1970.

DIJ-5 ———. "The Humble Programmer." *Communications of the ACM,* Vol. 15, No. 10 (October 1972), pp. 859-66. (See also [YOU-6].)

DIJ-6 ———. *A Discipline of Programming.* Englewood Cliffs, N.J.: Prentice-Hall, 1976.

DIJ-7 ———. "Structured Programming." *Software Engineering, Concepts and Techniques, Proceedings of the NATO Conferences,* eds. P. Naur, B. Randell, and J.N. Buxton. New York: Petrocelli/Charter, 1976, pp. 222-26. (See also [YOU-6].)

FAG-1 Fagan, M.E. "Design and Code Inspections to Reduce Errors in Program Development." *IBM Systems Journal,* Vol. 15, No. 3 (July 1976), pp. 182-211.

FLE-1     Flesch, R. *The Art of Plain Talk.* New York: Collier Books, 1946.

GAL-1     Galler, B., and A.J. Perlis. *A View of Programming Languages.* Reading, Mass.: Addison-Wesley, 1970.

GAN-1     Gane, C.P. "Structured Systems Analysis and the Training of Systems Analysts." *Proceedings of the GUIDE 43 Conference.* Chicago: GUIDE International Corp., 1976.

GAN-2     ———. "Structured Systems Analysis." *1977 Systems Forum.* Atlanta: Life Office Management Association, March 1977.

GAN-3     ———, and T. Sarson. *Structured Systems Analysis: Tools and Techniques.* New York: Improved System Technologies, Inc., 1977.

GAU-1     Gauthier, R., and S. Ponto. *Designing Systems Programs.* Englewood Cliffs, N.J.: Prentice-Hall, 1970.

GEL-1     Geller, D.P., and D.P. Freedman. *Structured Programming in APL.* Cambridge, Mass.: Winthrop, 1976.

GIL-1     Gilb, T. *Software Metrics.* Cambridge, Mass.: Winthrop, 1976.

GIL-2     Gildersleeve, T.R. *Decision Tables and Their Practical Application in Data Processing.* Englewood Cliffs, N.J.: Prentice-Hall, 1970.

GOR-1     Gorn, S. "Specification Languages for Mechanical Languages and Their Processors." *Communications of the ACM,* Vol. 4, No. 12 (December 1961), pp. 532-42.

HAL-1     Halstead, M.H. *Elements of Software Science.* New York: American Elsevier, 1977.

HER-1     Hermes, H. *Aufzählbarkeit, Entscheidbarkeit, Berechenbarkeit.* Berlin: Springer-Verlag, 1961.

HOA-1     Hoare, C.A.R. "An Axiomatic Approach to Computer Programming." *Communications of the ACM,* Vol. 12, No. 10 (October 1969), pp. 576-80, 583.

HOA-2 ———. "Proof of a Program: FIND." *Communications of the ACM,* Vol. 14, No. 1 (January 1971), pp. 39-45.

HOA-3 ———. *Hints for Programming Language Design.* Computer Science Report STAN-CS-7 4-403. Stanford, Calif.: Stanford University, January 1974.

IAN-1 Ianov, Y.I. "On the Equivalence and Transformation of Program Schemes." *Dokl. Akad. Nauk SSSR,* Vol. 113 (1957), pp. 39-42. (Russian)

JAC-1 Jackson, M.A. *Principles of Program Design.* New York: Academic Press, 1975.

JEN-1 Jensen, K., and N. Wirth. "PASCAL — User Manual and Report." *Lecture Notes in Computer Science,* Vol. 18. New York: Springer-Verlag, 1974.

JON-1 Jones, M. "Using HIPO to Develop Functional Specifications." *Datamation,* Vol. 22, No. 3 (March 1976), pp. 112-25.

KAI-1 Kain, W.J. "The Practice of Structured Analysis." *1977 Systems Forum.* Atlanta: Life Office Management Association, March 1977.

KAT-1 Katzan, H., Jr. *Systems Analysis and Documentation: An Introduction to the HIPO Method.* New York: Van Nostrand Reinhold, 1976.

KER-1 Kernighan, B.W., and P.J. Plauger. *The Elements of Programming Style.* New York: McGraw-Hill, 1974.

KER-2 ———. *Software Tools.* Reading, Mass: Addison-Wesley, 1976.

KER-3 Kernighan, B.W., and D.M. Ritchie. *The C Programming Language.* Englewood Cliffs, N.J.: Prentice-Hall, 1978.

KIN-1 King, J. "A Program Verifier." Ph.D. Thesis, Carnegie-Mellon Institute of Technology, 1969.

KNU-1 Knuth, D.E. "An Empirical Study of FORTRAN Programs." *Software — Practice and Experience,* Vol. 1, No. 2 (April-June 1971), pp. 105-33.

KNU-2 ⎯⎯⎯. "Structured Programming with go to Statements." *Current Trends in Programming Methodology,* Vol. I, ed. R.T. Yeh. Englewood Cliffs, N.J.: Prentice-Hall, 1977. (See also [YOU-6].)

KNU-3 ⎯⎯⎯, and R.W. Floyd. "Notes on Avoiding 'go to' Statements." *Information Processing Letters,* Vol. 1, No. 1 (February 1971), pp. 23-31.

LEA-1 Leavenworth, B.M. "Programming with(out) the GOTO." *Proceedings of the 1972 ACM Annual Conference.* New York: Association for Computing Machinery, August 1972, pp. 782-86.

LIS-1 Lister, T., and E. Yourdon. *Learning to Program in Structured COBOL, Part 2.* New York: YOURDON Press, 1978.

LOW-1 Lowry, E.S., and C.W. Medlock. "Object Code Optimization." *Communications of the ACM,* Vol. 12, No. 1 (January 1969), pp. 13-22.

LUC-1 Luckham, D.C., D.M.R. Park, and M.S. Paterson. "On Formalized Computer Programs." *Computer and System Sciences,* Vol. 4 (June 1970), pp. 220-49.

MAN-1 Manna, Z. "Termination of Algorithms." Ph.D. Thesis, Carnegie-Mellon Institute of Technology, 1968.

MAN-2 ⎯⎯⎯, S. Ness, and J. Vuillemin. "Inductive Methods for Proving Properties of Programs." *Communications of the ACM,* Vol. 16, No. 8 (August 1973), pp. 491-502.

MAR-1 Martin, J. *Computer Data-Base Organization,* 2nd ed. Englewood Cliffs, N.J.: Prentice-Hall, 1977.

MCC-1 McCabe, T.J. "A Complexity Measure." *IEEE Transactions on Software Engineering,* Vol SE-2 (December 1976).

MCC-2 McCarthy, J. "Recursive Functions of Symbolic Expressions and Their Computation by Machine, Part I." *Communications of the ACM,* Vol. 3, No. 4 (April 1960), pp. 184-95.

MCC-3    McCracken, D. *A Simplified Guide to Structured COBOL Programming.* New York: John Wiley & Sons, 1976.

MCG-1    McGowan, C.L., and J.R. Kelly. *Top-Down Structured Programming.* New York: Petrocelli/Charter, 1975.

MCH-1    McHenry, R.C. *Management Concepts for Top-Down Structured Programming.* IBM Corp., Report No. FSC 73-0001. Gaithersburg, Md.: IBM Federal Systems Div.; 1973.

MEA-1    Mealy, G.H. "Another Look at Data." *Proceedings of the 1967 AFIPS Fall Joint Computer Conference,* Vol. 31. Montvale, N.J.: AFIPS Press, 1967, pp. 525-34.

MIL-1    Miller, E.F., Jr. "Extensions to FORTRAN and Structured Programming — An Experiment." Report No. RM-1608. Santa Barbara, Calif.: General Research Corp., March 1972.

MIL-2    Miller, G.A. "The Magical Number Seven, Plus or Minus Two: Some Limits on Our Capacity for Processing Information." *Psychological Review,* Vol. 63 (March 1956), pp. 81-97.

MIL-3    Mills, H.D. "Top-Down Programming in Large Systems." *Debugging Techniques in Large Systems,* ed. R. Rustin. Englewood Cliffs, N.J.: Prentice-Hall, 1971, pp. 41-55.

MIL-4    _____. *Chief Programmer Teams: Principles and Procedures.* IBM Corp. Report No. FSC 71-5108. Gaithersburg, Md.: IBM Federal Systems Div., 1971.

MIL-5    _____. *Mathematical Foundations for Structured Programming.* IBM Corp. Report No. FSC 72-6012. Gaithersburg, Md.: IBM Federal Systems Div., 1972.

MYE-1    Myers, G.J. *Composite Design: The Design of Modular Programs.* IBM Corp. Technical Report TR00.2406. Poughkeepsie, N.Y.: IBM, January 1973.

MYE-2    _____. "Characteristics of Composite Design." *Datamation,* Vol. 19, No. 9 (September 1973), pp. 100-102.

MYE-3     _____. *Reliable Software Through Composite Design.* New York: Petrocelli/Charter, 1975.

NAU-1     Naur, P. "Proof of Algorithms by General Snapshots." *BIT,* Vol. 6, No. 4 (1966), pp. 310-16.

NAU-2     _____. "Programming by Action Clusters." *BIT,* Vol. 9, No. 3 (1969), pp. 250-58.

NAU-3     _____, B. Randell, and J.N. Buxton, eds. *Software Engineering, Concepts and Techniques, Proceedings of the NATO Conferences.* New York: Petrocelli/Charter, 1976.

NOL-1     Noll, P. *Structured Programming for the COBOL Programmer.* Fresno, Calif.: Mike Murach & Assoc., 1977.

ORR-1     Orr, K.T. *Structured Systems Development.* New York: YOURDON Press, 1977.

PAR-1     Parnas, D. "Information Distribution Aspects of Design Methodology." *Proceedings of the 1971 IFIP Congress.* Amsterdam, The Netherlands: North-Holland Publishing Co., 1972.

PAR-2     _____. "A Course on Software Engineering." *Proceedings of the ACM SIGCSE Technical Symposium,* March 1972.

PAR-3     _____. "A Technique for Software Module Specification with Examples." *Communications of the ACM,* Vol. 15, No. 5 (May 1972), pp. 330-36.

PAR-4     _____. "On the Criteria to Be Used in Decomposing Systems into Modules." *Communications of the ACM,* Vol. 15, No. 12 (December 1972), pp. 1053-58.

PAT-1     Paterson, M.S., and C.E. Hewitt. "Comparative Schematology." Unpublished memo.

PED-1     Pedersen, J., and J. Buckle, "Kongsberg's Road to an Industrial Software Methodology." *IEEE Transactions on Software Engineering,* Vol. SE-4, No. 4 (July 1978).

PET-1   Peter, R. "Graphschemata und Rekursive Funktionen." *Dialectica,* Vol. 12 (1958), pp. 373-93.

PLA-1   Plauger, P.J. "New York Times Revisited." *The YOURDON Report.* Vol. 1, No. 3 (April 1976), pp. 4-5.

REF-1   *IEEE Transactions on Software Engineering,* Vol. SE-3, No. 1 (January 1977). Entire issue devoted to Structured Analysis.

REF-2   *HIPO — Hierarchical Input-Process-Output Documentation Technique.* Audio Education Package, Form No. SR20-9413. Available through any IBM Branch Office.

REF-3   *HIPO: A Design Aid and Documentation Technique.* IBM Manual, Form GC20-1851-0. White Plains, N.Y.: IBM Data Processing Div., October 1974.

REF-4   *Proceedings of the Second International Conference on Software Engineering.* New York: IEEE Computer Society, October 1976.

REF-5   *The Bell System Technical Journal.* Vol. 57, No. 6 (July-August 1978), Part 2. Murray Hill, N.J.: Bell Laboratories, 1978.

RIG-1   Riguet, J. "Programmation et Théorie des Catégories." *Proceedings of the ICC Symposium on Symbolic Languages in Data Processing.* New York: Gordon and Breach, 1962, pp. 83-98.

ROS-1   Ross, D.T., and J.W. Brackett. "An Approach to Structured Analysis: An Analysis Technique Similar to Structured Programming Enables Systems to Be Designed More Effectively." *Computer Decisions,* Vol. 7, No. 9 (September 1976), pp. 40-44.

ROS-2   Ross, D.T., and K.E. Schoman, Jr. "Structured Analysis for Requirements Definition." *IEEE Transactions on Software Engineering,* Vol. SE-3, No. 1 (January 1977), pp. 6-15. (See also [YOU-6].)

SIM-1   Simpson, J. "Analysis and Design — A Case Study in a Structured Approach." *Australasian Computerworld,* Vol. 1, No. 2 (July 21, 1978), pp. 8-11, 13.

SOF-1   *Introduction to SADT.* SofTech Document No. 9022-78. Waltham, Mass.: SofTech Inc., February 1976.

STA-1   Stark, R. "A Language for Algorithms." *Computer Journal,* Vol. 14, No. 1 (February 1971), pp. 40-44.

STE-1   Stevens, W.G., G.J. Myers, and L.L. Constantine. "Structured Design." *IBM Systems Journal,* Vol. 13, No. 2 (May 1974), pp. 115-39. (See also [YOU-6].)

STR-1   Strong, H.R. "Translating Recursion Equations into Flowcharts." *Journal of Computer and System Sciences,* Vol. 5, No. 3 (June 1971), pp. 254-58.

SUL-1   Sullivan, J.E. *Extending PL/I for Structured Programming.* Report MTR-2353. Bedford, Mass.: Mitre Corp., March 1972.

TEI-1   Teichroew, D., and E.A. Hershey, III. "PSL/PSA: A Computer-Aided Technique for Structured Documentation and Analysis of Information Processing Systems." *IEEE Transactions on Software Engineering,* Vol. SE-3, No. 1 (January 1977), pp. 41-48. (See also [YOU-6].)

TEI-2   Teichroew, D., and H. Sayani. "Automation of System Building." *Datamation,* Vol. 17, No. 8 (1971), pp. 25-30.

WAL-1   Walston, C.E., and C.P. Felix. "A Method of Programming Measurement and Estimation." *IBM Systems Journal,* Vol 16, No. 1 (January 1977).

WAR-1   Warnier, J.D. *Logical Construction of Programs,* 3rd ed. New York: Van Nostrand Reinhold Co., 1974.

WEI-1   Weinberg, G.M. *PL/I Programming: A Manual of Style.* New York: McGraw-Hill, 1970.

WEI-2   _____. *The Psychology of Computer Programming.* New York: Van Nostrand Reinhold, 1971.

WEI-3   _____. *Structured Programming in PL/C.* New York: John Wiley & Sons, 1972.

WEI-4   _____. *An Introduction to General Systems Thinking.* New York: John Wiley & Sons, 1975.

WEI-5 _____, S.E. Wright, R. Kauffman, and M.A. Goetz. *High Level COBOL Programming.* Cambridge, Mass.: Winthrop, 1977.

WEI-6 Weinberg, V. *Structured Analysis.* New York: YOURDON Press, 1978.

WHI-1 Whitehouse, G.E. *Systems Analysis and Design Using Network Techniques.* Englewood Cliffs, N.J.: Prentice-Hall, 1973.

WIJ-1 van Wijngaarden, A. "Recursive Definition of Syntax and Semantics." *Formal Language Description Languages,* ed. T.B. Steel. Amsterdam, The Netherlands: North-Holland Publishing Co., 1966.

WIR-1 Wirth, N. "Program Development by Stepwise Refinement." *Communications of the ACM,* Vol. 14, No. 4 (April 1971), pp. 221-27.

WIR-2 _____. "The Programming Language Pascal." *Acta Informatica,* Vol. 1, No. 1 (1971), pp. 35-63.

WIR-3 _____. *Systematic Programming.* Englewood Cliffs, N.J.: Prentice-Hall, 1973.

WIR-4 _____. *Algorithms + Data Structures = Programs.* Englewood Cliffs, N.J.: Prentice-Hall, 1976.

WIR-5 _____, and C.A.R. Hoare. "A Contribution to the Development of ALGOL." *Communications of the ACM,* Vol. 9, No. 6 (June 1966), pp. 413-32.

WOO-1 Woodward, M.R., M.A. Hennell, and D. Hedley. "A Measure of Control Flow Complexity in Program Text." *IEEE Transactions on Software Engineering,* Vol SE-5, No. 1 (January 1979).

WUL-1 Wulf, W.A. "Programming Without the GOTO." *Proceedings of the 1971 IFIP Congress,* Vol. 1. Amsterdam, The Netherlands: North-Holland Publishing Co., 1972, pp. 408-13.

WUL-2 ———. "A Case Against the GOTO." *Proceedings of the 1972 Annual ACM Conference.* New York: Association for Computing Machinery, 1972, pp. 791-97. (See also [YOU-6].

WUL-3 ———, D.B. Russell, and A.N. Habermann. "BLISS: A Language for Systems Programming." *Communications of the ACM,* Vol. 14, No. 12 (December 1971), pp. 780-90.

WUL-4 ———, et al. "Reflections on a Systems Programming Language." *Proceedings of the SIGPLAN Symposium on Systems Implementation Languages.* New York: Association for Computing Machinery, October 1971.

YOU-1 Yourdon, E. "A Brief Look at Structured Programming and Top-Down Design." *Modern Data,* June 1974, pp. 30-35.

YOU-2 ———. *Techniques of Program Structure and Design.* Englewood Cliffs, N.J.: Prentice-Hall, 1975.

YOU-3 ———. "The Emergence of Structured Analysis." *Computer Decisions,* Vol. 8, No. 4 (April 1976), pp. 58-59.

YOU-4 ———. *Managing the Structured Techniques.* New York: YOURDON Press, 1979.

YOU-5 ———. *Structured Walkthroughs.* New York: YOURDON Press, 1977.

YOU-6 ———, ed. *Classics in Software Engineering.* New York: YOURDON Press, 1979.

YOU-7 ———, and L.L. Constantine. *Structured Design: Fundamentals of a Discipline of Computer Program and Systems Design.* Englewood Cliffs, N.J.: Prentice-Hall, 1979. (1979 edition of YOURDON's 1975 text)

YOU-8 ———, C. Gane, and T. Sarson. *Learning to Program in Structured COBOL, Part 1.* New York: YOURDON Press, 1976.

ZAH-1 Zahn, C.T. *C Notes: A Guide to the C Programming Language.* New York: YOURDON Press, 1979.